UNIVERSITY OF MINNESOTA

Ezra Pound

BY WILLIAM VAN O'CONNOR

UNIVERSITY OF MINNESOTA PRESS · MINNEAPOLIS

© Copyright 1963 by the University of Minnesota

Printed in the United States of America at
the North Central Publishing Company, St. Paul

Library of Congress Catalog Card Number: 63-62712

Distributed to high schools in the United States by
McGraw-Hill Book Company, Inc.
New York   Chicago   Corte Madera, Calif.   Dallas

PUBLISHED IN GREAT BRITAIN, INDIA, AND PAKISTAN BY THE OXFORD
UNIVERSITY PRESS, LONDON, BOMBAY, AND KARACHI, AND IN
CANADA BY THOMAS ALLEN, LTD., TORONTO

EZRA POUND

WILLIAM VAN O'CONNOR, an editor of the University of
Minnesota Pamphlets on American Writers, has written
literary criticism and fiction. He is a professor of
English at the University of California, Davis.

Ezra Pound

On the afternoon of December 7, 1941, Ezra Pound, a famous American literary expatriate, left his home in Rapallo, Italy, took a train for Rome, and over the state radio read the following:

"Europe calling. Pound speaking. Ezra Pound speaking, and I think I am perhaps speaking a bit more to England than to the United States, but you folks may as well hear it. They say an Englishman's head is made of wood and the American head made of watermelon. Easier to get something into the American head but nigh impossible to make it stick there for ten minutes. Of course, I don't know what good I am doing. I mean what immediate good, but some things you folks on both sides of the wretched ocean will have to learn, war or no war, sooner or later. Now, what I had to say about the state of mind in England in 1919, I said in Cantos 14 and 15. Some of your philosophists and fancy thinkers would have called it the spiritual side of England. I undertook to say state of mind.

"I can't say my remarks were heeded. I thought I got 'em simple enough. In fact, some people complained that several of the words contained no more than four or five letters, some six. Now I hold that no Catholic has ever been or ever will be puzzled by what I said in those Cantos. I have, however, never asked for any sympathy when misunderstood. I go on, try to make my meaning clear and then clearer, and in the long run, people who listen to me, very few of 'em do, but the members of that small and select minority do know more in the long run than those who listen to say H. G. (Chubby) Wells and the liberal stooges. What I am getting at is, a friend said to me the other day that he was glad I had the politics I have got but that he didn't understand how I, as a North American United Stateser, could have it. Well, that looks simple to me. On the Confucian system, very few start right and then go on, start at the roots and move upwards. The pattern often is simple. Whereas, if you start constructing from the twig downwards, you get into a muddle. My politics seem to me simple. My idea of a state or empire is more like a hedgehog or porcupine — chunky and well-defended. I don't cotton to the idea o' my country bein' an octopus, weak in the tentacles and suffering from stomach ulcers and colic gastritis."

For this, one of a hundred broadcasts, he was paid about ten dollars.

Pound's sentences and paragraphs suggest the disordered mind of a cracker-barrel sage. They do not sound like the work of a man who had made a career out of refining and purifying the English language, improving it as a vehicle for civilized discourse, or of the poet whom T. S. Eliot had called *il miglior fabbro*, the better craftsman. In fact, the broadcasts were so incomprehensible that the Italian government once took Pound off the air, suspecting him of sending code messages to the United States.

Pound (born in 1885) entered the University of Pennsylvania in 1901, but took his degree at Hamilton College. He returned to Pennsylvania for an M.A. At Pennsylvania he was friendly with William Carlos Williams and Hilda Doolittle. He spent a year in Europe before doing a teaching stint at Wabash College, in Indiana. The young Pound was a curious combination of Bohemian, scholar, and poet. He also saw himself as a very important teacher. In the early years of his career there were those who accepted Pound not merely as a poetic genius but as a writer who was revolutionizing English and American poetry. There is some justification for both of the latter claims.

There is also, however, a great deal of misunderstanding about Pound, and perhaps even misrepresentation. The fact is that in December 1945 Ezra Pound was declared insane. There can be no doubt that his rantings over the radio are mad. In this respect, they are not very different from some of the later *Cantos* and the later essays. The earliest prose, for example the fine study of Henry James, is perceptive and cogent, and the poetry written during the same period, mostly before World War I, is often carefully wrought and subtle. But even then, in the poetry, one is never wholly certain which of the Pound voices is the real Pound.

Pound the lyricist is most frequently in view, and it is in his lyricism that he has had his greatest success. This is best exhibited, perhaps, in the early *Cantos*. It appears intermittently, sometimes in explosive flashes, in the later *Cantos*, but usually the lyricism is not sustained; in its place one finds anecdotes, cryptic and gnomic utterances, dirty jokes, obscenities of various sorts, and a harsh insistence on the importance to culture of certain political leaders and economists.

The majority of Pound's critics find the *Cantos* his most important literary contribution. Various efforts have been made to say what they are about. Perhaps the easiest way of getting at their subject matter is to say they are about Pound's reactions to his own reading, of Homer, Ovid, or Remy de Gourmont, of various economists and political leaders, and Pound's own literary recollections, usually memories of London or Paris. As the years went by, Pound became less interested in literature than in economics, although he continued to express literary interests in the *Cantos*, and his interest in translating from Greek and Latin remained fairly constant.

After leaving London, in 1920, Pound became less and less a discoverer of true talents, and more and more the angry and, as he saw it, rejected prophet. Occasional successes in his poems and translations are reminiscent of the early genius and promise of Pound, but for the most part Pound's literary career was all down hill.

The young Pound had long wanted to meet William Butler Yeats, whom he believed to be the greatest poet of the previous one hundred years. In 1908, during his second trip abroad, they did meet. In London Pound set up a lecture course at the Regent Street Polytechnic, and here during the winter of 1908–9, he met Dorothy Shakespear and her mother Olivia Shakespear, friend of many literary men and in particular of Yeats. Pound and Yeats were to see a great deal of each other, drawn together by common interests and perhaps later by Pound's marriage to Dorothy Shakespear and Yeats's marriage to the daughter of Mrs. Shakespear's sister-in-law.

Personæ of Ezra Pound was published in 1909, and at least one reviewer found in it echoes of Yeats. The same year, Pound was advising Williams to read Yeats's essays, and Yeats was writing to his friend Lady Gregory that Pound's poetry is "definitely music, with strong marked time and yet it is effective speech." Sometimes their egos contended, as on the evening, according to fellow poet Ernest Rhys, a group went to the Old Cheshire Cheese, where Yeats held forth at length on the ways of bringing music and poetry together. Pound sought attention by eating two red tulips. When Yeats finished his monologue, Pound recited "Ballad of the Goodly Fere."

Pound was soon recognized as a literary figure of some eminence. In 1909 he became friendly with Ford Madox Hueffer (later Ford Madox Ford) and at one of the latter's parties met the young D. H. Lawrence. In 1910 he returned to the United States. After several months spent with his parents, Pound lived for a short time in

8

New York. He saw quite a bit of Yeats's father, John Butler Yeats, who was living and painting in New York, and Dr. Williams. He also strengthened his position as literary foreign correspondent, and when he returned to London he was busily officious writing advice to Harriet Monroe, editor of *Poetry*, and pontificating in literary groups. Pound's *Ripostes* was published in 1912. The widow of Ernest Fenollosa, having seen Pound's work in *Poetry*, brought him her husband's manuscripts. Fenollosa, a Bostonian, was the first Westerner to open up classical Japanese drama. Pound spent several years working on the plays. *Certain Noble Plays of Japan* was published, in 1916, by the Cuala Press, run by Yeats's sister, and Yeats wrote the introduction.

Reminiscences of the period, including those by Douglas Goldring, Richard Aldington, J. G. Fletcher, Conrad Aiken, Ernest Rhys, Wyndham Lewis, Ford Madox Ford, and many others, have amply testified to Pound's literary activities in London in the years before World War I.

William Carlos Williams, who visited London in 1910, recalled that Pound "lived the poet as few of us had the nerve to live that exalted role in our time." Having little money, he wore a fur-lined overcoat indoors and out during cold weather, and a broad-brimmed hat. Williams observed that Pound kept a candle lit before the picture of Dorothy Shakespear on his dresser. Pound as a dandified Bohemian was never offstage.

In May 1911 Pound wrote his father: "Yeats I like very much. I've seen him a great deal, almost daily. . . . He is, as I have said, a very great man, and he improves on acquaintance." In London Yeats lived at Woburn Place, off the Euston Road. Yeats believed his reputation was declining; he had digestive trouble and difficulties with his eyes. Pound attended to the older poet's needs, reading to him and instructing him in ways of being more "definite and concrete" in his poetry. Pound sometimes organized dinners for literary people, then took them to Woburn Place, where Yeats held forth.

In 1912, Pound altered, without permission, some poems Yeats had given him to send to *Poetry*. Yeats was infuriated, but then forgave the bumptious and arrogant young Pound. Pound had set out to make Yeats more modern. During the winters of 1913–14, 1914–15, and 1915–16 he acted as "Uncle William's secretary" at a small house, Stone Cottage, in Sussex. Pound wrote his mother that he regarded the job "as a duty to posterity." When Pound married, he brought his wife to live at Stone Cottage. Yeats enjoyed hearing the young couple discuss modern critical doctrines. He was not enthusiastic about *des imagistes* with whom Pound was closely associated, but admitted their "satiric intensity." In 1916 Yeats handed over his father's letters for Pound to edit for the Cuala Press, saying he represented "the most aggressive contemporary school of the young."

Pound's revisions of Yeats's poetry were in the direction of conciseness and clarity. A revision from the later years perhaps illustrates the nature of the changes. This is from a draft of "From the Antigone":

> Overcome, O bitter sweetness,
> The rich man and his affairs,
> The fat flocks and the fields' fatness,
> Mariners, wild harvesters;
> Overcome Gods upon Parnassus;
> Overcome the Empyrean; hurl
> Heaven and Earth out of their places —
> Inhabitant of the soft cheek of a girl
> And into the same calamity
> That brother and brother, friend and friend,
> Family and family,
> City and city may contend
> By that great glory driven wild —
> Pray I will and sing I must

> And yet I weep — Oedipus' child
> Descends into the loveless dust.

Pound made the eighth line follow the first, substituted "That in" for "And into" in the ninth line, and dropped "that" from the tenth line. Thus the poem was made to read:

> Overcome — O bitter sweetness,
> Inhabitant of the soft cheek of a girl —
> The fat flocks and the field's fatness . . .
> > hurl
> Heaven and Earth out of their places,
> That in the same calamity
> Brother and brother, friend and friend,
> Family and family,
> City and city may content . . .

Without question, Pound's changes greatly improve the poem.

On one occasion, in the winter of 1914, Pound organized a small group of poets to honor Wilfrid Scawen Blunt, then seventy-four. The poets were Sturge Moore, Victor Plarr, Frederic Manning, F. S. Flint, Richard Aldington, and Yeats. A dinner was held at Blunt's estate. Pound presented Blunt a marble box carved by Gaudier-Brzeska, containing poems by all the poets. Pound also read an address honoring Blunt. The latter replied; then Yeats talked about the state of poetry, saying those who came to honor Blunt represented different schools. "To Sturge Moore, for instance, the world is impersonal. . . . Pound has a desire personally to insult the world. He has a volume of manuscript at present in which his insults to the world are so deadly that it is a rather complicated publishing problem." Writing Canto LXXXI, years later, Pound recalled the occasion, saying it was not vanity to have taken the pains to honor Blunt —

> To have gathered from the air a live tradition
> or from a fine old eye the unconquered flame.

One may say the same for Pound's relationship with Yeats. Pound took from the air a live tradition. And Yeats sloughed off more and more of the 1890's. Perhaps it was Pound's work on the Japanese Noh plays, as much as anything, that helped Yeats discover a new direction, at least gave him a new kind of symbolic action. His *The Hawk's Well*, founded on the Noh, was performed at Lady Cunard's house in Cavendish Square, April 2, 1916. Seeing the play changed Eliot's view of Yeats: "Yeats was well-known, of course; but to me, at least, Yeats did not appear, until after 1917 [he should say, 1916], to be anything but a minor survivor of the 90's. After that date, I saw him very differently. I remember clearly my impression of the first performance of *The Hawk's Well*, in a London drawing room, with a celebrated Japanese dancer in the role of the hawk, to which Pound took me. And thereafter one saw Yeats rather as a more eminent contemporary than an elder from whom one could learn."

Conrad Aiken had introduced Eliot to Pound in 1915. Eliot was unable to find an editor willing to accept any of his poems. Pound admired Eliot's work, and sent "Prufrock" to *Poetry*. It caused at least a mild sensation, helped to get the modernist movement underway, and launched Eliot's career. Pound edited *Catholic Anthology* (1915) for the purpose, he said, of getting sixteen pages of Eliot into print at once. Also through Pound's efforts Eliot's first volume of poems was published in 1917 by the Egoist Press.

Eliot remembers Pound's quarters at 5 Holland Place, "a small dark flat in Kensington." Because of his restless energy and fidgety manner, Pound struck Eliot as ready for some new move or involvement. "In America, he would no doubt have seemed on the point of going abroad; in London, he always seemed on the point of crossing the Channel."

Pound's attitude toward the United States and, by implication, his hopes and ambitions for himself can be seen in *Patria Mia*, written in 1913 but unpublished until 1950. A publisher in Chicago, to whom it had been sent, lost the manuscript, and it was recovered, more than a generation later, when the firm moved to new quarters. Between 1913 and 1950 Pound had lived in Paris and Rapallo, witnessed two wars, published innumerable articles and books, been indicted for treason and imprisoned in an institution for the insane for several years. *Patria Mia* sheds light on Pound's career in the years following its composition. It is not as incoherent as his later books and pamphlets on politics and economics, but it rambles and is certainly not the tightly organized argument Pound believed he was writing. It also suggests the disappointment he would suffer.

Pound, in *Patria Mia*, is giving advice to America. He says, for example, what changes should be made in American colleges and graduate schools, and how magazine editorial policies should be altered. The underlying theme of each of his suggestions is that a genuine poet — and he would not have had to go far to find one — should be hired to stimulate academic life or give the right sort of advice to editors.

Pound's essential criticism of America repeats what Henry James said in *The American Scene* (1907), that Americans were obsessed by money and material acquisitions. Pound wrote: "It is not strange, for every man, or practically every man, with enough mental energy to make him interesting is engaged in either business or politics. And our politics are by now no more than a branch of business." A detailed comparison of *Patria Mia* and *The American Scene* might prove useful. Probably it would show that James's perceptiveness as well as his capacity for coherently ordering his impressions and arguments greatly transcended Pound's.

Curiously, Pound's affection for America comes through strongly. After his visit, James had to return to Rye in England to compose himself. Something in Pound responds to the vigor and rawness of America. One finds him, for example, saying New York City is probably the most beautiful city in the world:

"And New York is the most beautiful city in the world?

"It is not far from it. No urban nights are like the nights there. I have looked down across the city from high windows. It is then that the great buildings lose reality and take on their magical powers. They are immaterial; that is to say one sees but the lighted windows.

"Squares after squares of flame, set and cut into the aether. Here is our poetry, for we have pulled down the stars to our will.

"As for the harbour, and the city from the harbour. A huge Irishman stood beside me the last time I went back there and he tried vainly to express himself by repeating: —

" 'It uccedes Lundun.'

" 'It uccedes Lundun.'

"I have seen Cadiz from the water. The thin, white lotus beyond a dazzle of blue. I know somewhat of cities. The Irishman thought of size alone. I thought of the beauty, and beside it Venice seems like a tawdry scene in a play-house. New York is out of doors.

"And as for Venice; when Mr. Marinetti and his friends [a "modernist" group] shall have succeeded in destroying that ancient city, we will rebuild Venice on the Jersey mud flats and use the same for a tea-shop."

Pound has great hopes for America. The millionaires and industrialists will be obliged to subsidize the arts, just as wealthy merchants and princes had during the Renaissance. He believes they will do this. Pound also says that when an American investigating "in any art or *metier* has learned what is the best, he will never after be content with the second-rate. It is by this trait that we are a young nation and a strong one. An old nation weighs the cost of the best, and asks if the best is worth while."

Pound tries to isolate American qualities. He cites "a certain generosity," "a certain carelessness, or looseness," "a hatred of the sordid," a "desire for largeness," and "a willingness to stand exposed." He feels these qualities in Whitman —

> Camerado, this is no book,
> Who touches this touches a man.

Pound dismisses Whitman because he is not a craftsman, not an artist, but at the same time makes him an American symbol: "Whitman established the national *timbre*. One may not need him at home. It is in the air, this tonic of his. But if one is abroad; if one is ever likely to forget one's birth-right, to lose faith, being surrounded by disparagers, one can find, in Whitman, the reassurance. Whitman goes bail for the nation."

Pound deplores the genteel tradition, although he does not refer to it as such. He deplores the practice of editors of the *Atlantic* and other magazines (he cites Howells by name) of running imitations from the Greek Anthology, regular in meters and optimistic in attitude. They do not ask, he says, whether a poem is the work of a serious artist, whether the form is in accordance with the subject and the author's intention, or whether the idiom is the inevitable expression of a generation's collective view. At one point he refers to Coleridge's doctrine of organic form.

America can, he adds, produce genuine art. He says James was a true novelist, in the school of Flaubert and Turgenev, and a diagnostician "of all that is fine in American life." His second example is the painter Whistler, who "proved once and for all . . . that being born an American does not eternally damn a man or prevent him from the ultimate and highest achievement in the arts."

Considering Pound's long years in Europe, and his later attacks on American society and culture, *Patria Mia* is a strange book. In one place Pound wrote: "If a man's work require him to live in exile, let him suffer, or enjoy, his exile gladly. But it would be about as easy for an American to become a Chinaman or a Hindoo as for him to acquire an Englishness, or a Frenchness, or a European-ness that is more than half a skin deep."

Eliot observed Pound's passion to teach, saying he was reminded of Irving Babbitt, who also had a passion for giving people the right doctrines to believe. Eliot adds that the two men might have appeared even more alike if Pound had stayed at home and become a professor. And since he wrote this in 1946, Eliot might be implying that if Pound had been connected with an American university his mental health might have been better and he would not have managed to get into so much trouble.

Pound, however, had an enormous talent for getting into trouble. Wyndham Lewis' theory about Pound and England is fairly simple, and may well be true. English literary life, he said, was filled with well-educated amateurs. They resisted Pound's "fierce quest for perfection," and besides they disliked Americans. By 1918 Pound had grown into a "prickly, aloof, rebel mandarin." Pound, he says, "knew his England very well," but refused to "come to terms with it." He did what he had to do — he moved across the Channel to Paris.

But first a look at some of Pound's many concerns during his English period.

Between 1908 and 1920, Pound edited anthologies and contributed to them translations from various languages, and wrote his own poetry. During this period, which probably was the high point of his career as a poet and of his influence on other poets, he published at least fourteen volumes of poetry. What sort of poet was he in those years? As usual in discussing Pound, there can be no simple answer. Wyndham Lewis tries to say why: "Ezra Pound, I feel, is probably a poet of a higher and rarer order than it is easy at all times to realise, because of much irrelevant dust kicked up by his personality as it rushes, strides, or charges across the temporal scene." Also, the poetry is very uneven, and Pound writes in different voices.

Pound could be a sort of Sinclair Lewis, blasting the amenities of the genteel tradition. In "L'Homme Moyen Sensuel," for example, he wrote:

> Still I'd respect you more if you could bury
> Mabie, and Lyman Abbot and George Woodberry,
> For minds so wholly founded upon quotations
> Are not the best of pulse for infant nations. . . .

While he was in England, he would take similar swipes at anyone or any expression that threatened his notions of perfection in verse or any of his various critical theories. In these years Pound's blasts sometimes had verve and resonance; in later years they would often be harsh and vituperative.

R. P. Blackmur has made a good point about Pound as poet. He compares "Hugh Selwyn Mauberley" with "Homage to Sextus Propertius." The former — a series of related poems about a figure much like Pound himself who is critical of his milieu and is offering advice on how poetry should be written — he finds clever, the work of an excellent craftsman. The things the poem "says" are not very original or they are the usual complaints of the exiled poet, looking out from his *tour d'ivoire*. Oddly, it is as "translator" that Pound is original. Blackmur points out that Pound does not translate Propertius; he presents an English equivalent. For example, when Propertius writes, "Let verse run smoothly, polished with fine pumice," Pound writes, "We have to keep our erasers in order." Propertius writes, "Narrow is the path that leads to

1 7

the Muses"; Pound writes, "And there is no high-road to the Muses."

Pound is not especially imaginative in creating the substance of his own poems. His gift is verbal, and he is at his best when using another poet's substance for his own purposes. In the *Cantos*, as we shall see, he is not quite a translator, but he does rely on the substance of earlier poems.

F. R. Leavis has emphasized Pound's wit, especially in "Hugh Selwyn Mauberley." He finds the "verse is extraordinarily subtle," says that "critical activity accompanies feeling," and finds the poem "serious and light at the same time, sardonic and poignant, flippant and intense"; "Mauberley," he concludes, is a "great poem." John Espey in *Ezra Pound's Mauberley* has studied the poem brilliantly and with a detailed attention, especially to sources, probably never before given a poem. One's response to this sort of exegesis could be, *Now, really, ought not a poem so obviously witty, poised, critical, etc., give up its secrets more easily?* Perhaps the answer would be that the odd bits of arcana in Pound's mind are of such a nature that one must studiously search them out before being able to respond fully to his wit, grace, and critical poise. In other words, one has to decide whether the finished poem justifies a special course of study in preparation for reading it.

There is, as indicated earlier, yet another side to Pound's poetry, its lyricism. This will probably prove to be his greatest strength. In *The Translations of Ezra Pound* there are about seventy pages of poems translated from Provençal and Italian poets. All of these translations are lyrics.

During the years when Pound was leading the modernist revolt he was also writing poems from older literary conventions. A few lines from " 'Blandula, Tenulla, Vagula' " will serve as an example:

> What has thou, O my soul, with paradise?
> Will we not rather, when our freedom's won,
> Get us to some clear place wherein the sun
> Lets drift in on us through the olive leaves

This has the lyric force, though not the meditative quality and natural colors, of Wallace Stevens' "Sunday Morning," one of the great poems of our age, and a sustained performance probably beyond Pound at any stage of his career.

Another characteristic early lyric is "Erat Hora." It exhibits Pound's preoccupation with light as a symbol of love, beauty, and mutability.

> Nay, whatever comes
> One hour was sunlit and the most high gods
> May not make boast of any better thing
> Than to have watched that hour as it passed.

Pound is commonly seen as one who explained, justified, and rationalized the modernist idiom in poetry. All this is true. He has also written in that idiom. But at his best, as in occasional passages in the *Cantos*, he is a lyricist in the company of Herrick, Waller, or Ben Jonson, though certainly of a lesser order. His "translations" from Chinese poetry have a similar lyric quality. "The River Merchant's Wife: A Letter," written in a subdued tone, is as beautiful as any poem in the Pound canon.

In literary histories, however, Pound is usually treated as an Imagist or Vorticist. He was involved with both Imagism and Vorticism, but the nature of his involvement is a somewhat complicated story. In 1909, Pound had been introduced to a group led by T. E. Hulme that met regularly in a Soho restaurant to talk about poetry. He read "Sestina Altaforte" in tones that brought all eyes in the room to astonished attention. It was this group that began the Imagist movement, but within a year it broke up. There was a second group, in 1910, which also lasted about a year.

T. E. Hulme, a Cambridge man, a poet of sorts and a philosopher, was the dominating figure. He was a hard-living man, given to violence. He was killed later in the war. Hulme was skeptical, but willing to analyze as well as scoff. At the Soho meetings, on Thursdays, over spaghetti and wine, Hulme expounded his ideas. Poetry, he said, was lost in romantic smoothness, vagueness, fatuousness, and general insipidity. He wanted a period of dry, hard verse. Poetry needed a new convention. Man, he also said, was a limited creature. One need not descend a deep well to plumb his depths; a bucket would do!

In *Ripostes* Pound printed five of Hulme's poems. "In publishing his *Complete Poetical Works* at thirty," Pound wrote, "Mr Hulme has set an enviable example to many of his contemporaries who have had less to say. They are reprinted here for good fellowship; for good custom, a custom out of Tuscany and of Provence; and thirdly, for convenience, seeing their smallness of bulk; and for good memory, seeing that they recall certain evenings and meetings of two years gone, dull enough at the time, but rather pleasant to look back upon."

F. S. Flint and others have said that Pound did not establish the Imagist movement — he promoted it. Flint said the Hulme group assumed the need for experiment and studied Japanese, Hebrew, and French Symbolists, always giving close attention to imagery. Pound, according to Flint, was studying troubadour poetry and the discussions interested him only when he could relate them to troubadour poetry. In one of his essays Pound wrote: "I think the artist should master all known forms and systems of metric, and I have with some persistence set about doing this, searching particularly into those periods wherein the systems came to birth or attained their maturity." It is true that Pound was studying troubadour poetry but he was also studying music, art (he especially promoted the sculptor Gaudier-Brzeska), the relationship of prose to poetry, and Oriental drama and poetry, among other things.

Rhythms in music and poetry were a fairly constant preoccupation with Pound. Rhythm, he said, determines pitch and melody; pitch depends on the frequency with which sounds strike the ear; variations in pitch control melody. In poetry, he continued, the frequency of vowel or consonant sounds produces pitch; a changed frequency makes for higher or lower sound, and variation produces the melody of a line. Pound wrote articles and talked volubly about this and related observations, after he had met Arnold Dolmetsch and read his book, *The Interpretation of Music of the XVIIth and XVIIIth Centuries.* In one article he quotes from one of Dolmetsch's eighteenth-century sources, François Couperin, *L'Art de toucher le Clavecin* (1717): "I find that we confuse Time, or Measure, with what is called Cadence or Movement. Measure defines the quantity and equality of the beats; Cadence is properly the spirit, the soul that must be added." There seems to be nothing revolutionary in this, but Pound uses it to whip the vers libre movement. "It is too late to prevent *vers libre.* But, conceivably, one might improve it, and one might stop at least a little of the idiotic and narrow discussion based on an ignorance of music." He sees Couperin as justification for saying true vers libre ("You must bind perfectly what you play") was in the old music. Pound also quoted Eliot: *"Vers libre* does not exist. . . . There is no escape from metre; there is only mastery of it."

Another considerable influence on Pound was Ford Madox Ford (he was Ford Madox Hueffer until World War I), who had been a close associate of Conrad and James. In 1935, Pound wrote Dr. Williams: "I did Fordie as much justice as anyone (or almost anyone) did — but still not enough! Fordie knew more about writing than any of 'them' or 'us.' "

Ford belonged to what he called the Impressionist tradition. A scene is described and reacted to — it exists in the descriptions and in the vividness of the reaction. But the reaction is aesthetic, not didactic. He avoided a poetic stance, or being "literary." He used the "language of my own day," frequently a kind of prose, "to register my own times in terms of my own times." Especially, he said, poetry should be a response to life, not to books. (It is odd that Pound should single this out, since his own response is largely to books.)

Pound contributed a fairly long article to *Poetry*, entitled "Mr. Hueffer and the Prose Tradition," during the same year he issued *Des Imagistes*, a collection of poems by the Imagists. Pound refers to Stendhal's remark that prose was a higher form than poetry, and says Mr. Hueffer is a distinguished prose writer. He finds Hueffer a fine poet, saying "On Heaven" is "the best poem yet written in the 'twentieth-century fashion.' " Hueffer believed "poetry should be written at least as well as prose." Pound says Hueffer's poetry is "revolutionary," because of an "insistence upon clarity and precision, upon the prose tradition." The prose influence on modern poetry has been considerable, and one might reasonably infer that Pound's comments as well as his own practice were a considerable influence on other poets.

Before 1912, Pound had little to say about images, but thereafter he had much to say. Among Pound's "discoveries" were Hilda Doolittle ("H. D.") and Richard Aldington. In talking to them about their poetry he called them *imagistes*. In *Ripostes* he connected *des imagistes* and the "group of 1909." (Later, in 1939, Pound minimized the Hulme influence, and emphasized Ford's.) In 1913, in *Poetry*, Pound published "A Few Don'ts" and defined the Image: "An 'Image' is that which presents an intellectual and emotional complex in an instant of time. I use the word 'complex' rather in the technical sense employed by the newer psychologists . . . It is the presentation of such a 'complex' instantaneously which gives that sense of sudden liberation; that sense of freedom from time limits and space limits; that sense of sudden growth, which we experience in the presence of the greatest works of art."

Other magazines followed *Poetry* in promoting Imagism. Al-fred Kreymborg had asked for contributions to his magazine, the *Glebe*, and Pound sent him poems by Aldington, H. D., Flint, Hueffer, Williams, Connell, Lowell, Upward, Cournos, and James Joyce. *Des Imagistes* received a lot of attention in the United States, but in England, published by Harold Monro, it was a bust. Amy Lowell, in London, wanted to do a new anthology of Imagist poetry. Pound insisted on being editor, but she fought him and won. Thereafter the movement became what he called "Amy-gism."

Besides, Pound was in a new movement and associating with painters and sculptors. It was called Vorticism. Wyndham Lewis, Gaudier-Brzeska, and Pound were the guiding spirits. *Blast*, edited by Lewis, appeared in 1914. Two of the principles governing its policy were developed from earlier Pound statements: one, the necessity for a vigorous impact ("The vortex is the point of maxi-mum energy"), and, two, recognition of the image as "the primary pigment of poetry." A long Imagist poem is not possible because the image is a vortex "from which, through which, and into which, ideas are constantly rushing." A poem has a visual basis, and makes the intangible concrete. The doctrine seems remark-ably close to the one he had stated in *Poetry*.

Pound's interest in the image also derived from his deep in-volvement with Fenollosa's manuscripts, on Chinese as well as Japanese literature. As "Hugh Selwyn Mauberley" suggests, Pound felt a kinship with the poets of the 1890's. He was also very taken with Whistler; in fact, the first poem Pound published in *Poetry* (October 1912) was "To Whistler, American." From Whistler he took the idea of "poetry as picture." In "Au Jardin"

23

there are lines such as these: "she danced like a pink moth in the shrubbery" and "From amber lattices upon the cobalt night."

In his September 1914 article in the *Fortnightly Review* on Vorticism he says he wrote a hokku-like sentence:

'The apparition of these faces in a crowd;
Petals on a wet, black bough.'

He quotes a well-known hokku —

The fallen blossom flies back to its branch:
A butterfly.

Pound recognized in studying this that a descriptive or sometimes lyrical passage was followed by a vivid image. Earl Miner, the closest student of Japanese influences on Pound, calls this the "super pository method." Pound was to employ this technique frequently; for example, in these lines from the lovely "Liu Ch'e":

There is no sound of foot-fall, and the leaves
Scurry into heaps and lie still,
And she the rejoicer of the heart is beneath them:

A wet leaf that clings to the threshold.

Other notable examples are "A Song of the Degrees," "Ts'ai Chih," "Coitus," "The Encounter," "Fish and Shadow," and "Cantus Planis." One also finds the super pository method employed in the *Cantos*. In using the Chinese written characters, or ideograms, which he does in certain *Cantos*, Pound believed his method was similar to the super pository — use of a vivid image causing many of the preceding elements to cohere. However, since few of his readers understand the ideograms it is difficult to accept Pound's insistence on using them.

Miner says that Arthur Waley's *The Nō Plays of Japan* is the authoritative scholarly translation; the Pound-Fenollosa version is often unscholarly and based on misunderstanding of the historical contexts. Occasional passages, he adds, are beautifully executed. Although Pound's efforts with the Noh were not generally successful, he did learn things that contributed to his theory of the image.

In a note at the end of *Suma Genji*, Pound said the Noh has "what we may call Unity of Image . . . the red maple leaves and the snow flurry in *Nishikigi*, the pines in *Takasago*, the blue-grey waves and wave pattern in *Suma Genji*, the mantle of feathers in the play of that name, *Hagoromo*." The Noh gave Pound suggestions for organizing poems longer than the haiku, or hokku, or concise imagistic poems. Frequently in the *Cantos* Pound juxtaposes legends from Greek and Japanese sources, scenes from different cultures, and various heroes or villains, all in a seemingly haphazard way. Then he employs an image, or metaphor (a term he apparently chose not to use), that discovers a theme or essence common to the hitherto disparate elements.

Thus Pound's involvement with the image is not a simple matter.

Especially through Whistler and Théophile Gautier he felt the pull of the "Art for Art's Sake" movement. Pound was an aesthete. His commitment to Imagism and Vorticism was complicated by his interest in Chinese poetry and the Japanese Noh. Pound also theorized about the relationship between music (in the British *Who's Who* he identified himself as "poet and composer") and the conversational or prose line. On one occasion he had provided his contemporaries with a little anthology of nineteenth-century French poets, Baudelaire, Verlaine, Laforgue, the Symbolists. Their influence on Eliot, however, was greater than it was on Pound. The city, the automobile, and social life did not deeply engage him. There is a sense then in which Pound is not a modernist poet. Or perhaps one should say he was a modernist only briefly. Pound has a pantheon of writers who helped sustain his vision of the world as it ought to be, and more and more he turned to them.

During the English period, Pound studied Propertius, Arnaut Daniel, Dante, Cavalcanti, Stendhal, Flaubert, Gautier, James, and many others. The writers who did not interest Pound reveal strange deficiencies in his views of human conduct and in his own sensibilities. Joseph Conrad does not loom very large, and "them Rooshans," as he called them, go almost unmentioned. Tolstoi, Dostoevski, and Chekhov were uninteresting to Pound.

Three writers, Remy de Gourmont, Ovid, especially in Golding's translation of the *Metamorphoses*, and Robert Browning seem to have held pre-eminence in his pantheon. One might guess that Gourmont and Ovid, more than any other writers, satisfy Pound's dream of the world, and help him create his imaginary Great Good Place. Browning he likes for other reasons: for his craftsmanship, and apparently for writing poetry so much like Pound's own. He especially likes Browning for having written *Sordello*, the poem that made possible the *Cantos*, in which one finds exquisitely beautiful lyric passages, vivid imagistic scenes, tags from many languages, and Pound's racist and economic theories.

Pound several times links the names of Ovid, Propertius, and Remy de Gourmont. He quotes Propertius as saying: *Ingenium nobis ipsa puella facit.* In "Remy de Gourmont, A Distinction," he says: "Gourmont's wisdom is not wholly unlike the wisdom which those ignorant of Latin may, if the gods favor their understanding, derive from Golding's *Metamorphoses*."

Gourmont (1858–1915) profoundly impressed Pound. In the months before Gourmont's death, Pound was in correspondence with him about contributing to an international journal. Gourmont replied that he was exhausted, sick, and probably would not be of any great help in Pound's enterprise; he also doubted that Americans were "capable of enough mental liberty to read my books." However, he was willing to let Pound help them try to "respect French individualism," and "the sense of liberty which some of us have in so great degree."

In the essay cited above, Pound says, "Gourmont prepared our era." As in most of his other essays, Pound generalizes for a page or two, sets up a thesis, points out the writer's special contributions to civilized understanding, quotes copiously, lists bibliography, then clouts the reader on the back of the head, telling him to pay closer attention.

Gourmont does not, Pound says, "grant the duality of body and soul, or at least suggests that this medieval duality is unsatisfactory." James, whom Pound contrasts with Gourmont, intellectualized passion; emotions to him "were more or less things other people had and that one didn't go into." Sex in Gourmont's works is pervasive, like a drop of dye in a clear jar of water. Sex is related to sensibilities, and therefore to "the domain of aesthetics." This belief was back of Gourmont's concern with resonance in expressing emotion; knowing that ideas have little value apart from the modality of the mind receiving them, he differentiated characters by the modes of their sensibilities.

Gourmont's thesis is that man is a sensual creature, and should not be intimidated by the Christian teachings about modesty, chastity, and so on. Voluptuousness and sensual pleasure are their own excuse for being.

Gourmont's *Physique de l'Amour*, which Pound translated, is filled with such remarks as this: "Il y aurait peut-être une certain corrélation entre la copulation complète et profonde et le développement cérébral." A great deal of biological lore is exhibited, all of it focused on the sex habits of insects, fish, birds, and animals.

Probably Gourmont felt he was writing an amusing and mildly

titillating essay on man in nature. Pound, in a postscript, is less playful, and develops a thesis that "the brain itself is, in origin and development, only a sort of great clot of genital fluid held in suspense or reserve. . . ." Pound offers no scientific information to justify his theory. He is creating a little myth. There need be no quarrel between "cerebralist and viveur," he says, "if the brain is thus conceived not as a separate and desiccated organ, but as the very fluid of life itself."

Gourmont and Pound were both interested in Provençal poetry, in late Latin poets, and in literary eroticism. John Espey says that many sections and stanzas of "Hugh Selwyn Mauberley" bear witness to Pound's reading of Gourmont. Pound's earliest pieces on Gourmont appeared in 1913. Evidences of Gourmont's influence appear, for example, in the unabashed sexuality of Canto xxxix. Pound's admiration for Gourmont never changed. He refers admiringly to him in *Jefferson and/or Mussolini* (1935) and elsewhere. When Gourmont died, Pound wrote: "his thoughts had the property of life. They, the thoughts, were all related to life, they were immersed in the manifest universe while he thought them, they were not cut out, put on shelves and in bottles." Over the years in one form or another, Pound continued to repeat this; it is an expression of his doctrine, *make it new*.

Early and late in his career, Pound praises Ovid — "there is great wisdom in Ovid." In 1934, from Rapallo, in making up a reading list for a correspondent, he wrote: "There are a few things out of print. Golding's translation of Ovid's *Metamorphoses,* CERTAINLY . . . and being an institution of learning yr. Eng. prof. will never have heard of it; though it was good enough for Wm. Shakespear. *And* any dept. of English is a farce without it." Elsewhere he uses Golding's translation to berate Milton's Latinity, contrasting the former's natural "contemporary speech" with Milton's "vague pompous words." The quality of translations, he says, decreased as "translators ceased being interested in the subject matter of their original."

Golding's Ovid has some charm, if only because of its studied innocence and naiveté. If Golding falls short of greatness, as he does, he manages a difficult meter about as well as could be expected. For example,

> The Damsels at the sight of man quite out of
> countnance dasht,
> (Bicause they everichone were bare and naked
> to the quicke)
> Did beate their handes against their brests,
> and cast out such a shricke,
> That all the wood did ring thereof: and cling-
> ing to their dame
> Did all they could to hide both hir and eke
> themselves for shame.

It seems unlikely that Pound was greatly influenced by Golding's language, or his ingenuous playfulness. Pound's *Metamorphoses* is more "distanced," calmer, and seen in lights and shadows. There can be no doubt that he responds at some very deep level to the *Metamorphoses*. Gilbert Murray's account of Ovid's "vision" is a prose equivalent to what Pound tries to catch in his poetry. "What a world it is that he has created in the *Metamorphoses*! It draws its denizens from all the boundless resources of Greek mythology, a world of live forests and mountains and rivers, in which every plant and flower has a story and nearly always a love story; where the moon is indeed not a moon but an orbèd maiden, and the Sunrise weeps because she is still young and her belovèd is old; and the stars are human souls; and the Sun sees human virgins in the depths of forests and almost swoons at their beauty and pursues them; and other virgins, who feel the same way about him, commit great sins from jealousy . . . and turn into flowers; and all the youths and maidens are indescribably beautiful and adventurous and passionate . . . A world of wonderful children where nobody is really cross or wicked except the grown-ups; Juno, for instance . . . His criticism of life is very slight."

Robert Browning, as was observed earlier, was another of Pound's culture heroes. In his usual fashion of reordering literary history in a sentence or two, Pound has said the decline of England began on the day Landor packed his bags and moved to Tuscany. Thereafter Shelley, Keats, Byron, Beddoes lived on the Continent. Later there was "the edifying spectacle of Browning in Italy and Tennyson in Buckingham Palace." Pound admired in Browning many of the virtues he saw in Crabbe — realism, precision, terseness, the charged line, objectivity. And perhaps Pound's affection for Italy is involved with Browning's love for that country. On a number of occasions Pound had advised perplexed readers of the *Cantos* to take a good look at *Sordello*.

A passage in Book Two of *Sordello* seems to have suggested the method of the *Cantos*. The troubadour Sordello is musing on the delights of reading:

> — had he ever turned, in fact
> From Elys, to sing Elys? — from each fit
> Of rapture to contrive a song of it?
> True, this snatch or the other seemed to wind
> Into a treasure, helped himself to find
> A beauty in himself; for, see, he soared
> By means of that mere snatch, to many a hoard
> Of fancies; as some falling cone bears soft
> The eye along the fir-tree spire, aloft
> To a dove's nest. . . .
> Have they [men] fancies —
> slow, perchance,
> Not at their beck, which indistinctly glance
> Until, by song, each floating part be linked
> To each, and all grow palpable, distinct!
> He pondered this.

Pound found in *Sordello* a method that would allow him to muse upon and re-create his readings.

The first three *Cantos* appeared in *Poetry*, June, July, August 1917. In the June 1917 Canto I, subsequently dropped, Pound addresses Browning affectionately as "Bob Browning," telling him *Sordello* is an "art-form" and adding the modern world needs such a "rag-bag" in which to toss "all its thought." It does not matter, he says, that the anachronisms in *Sordello* are egregious — a poem should create a sense of life. He proposes to give up the "intaglio method," presumably the images associated with *des imagistes* and haiku, and enter a timeless fictional world — "you mix your eras," peopled by soldiers with robes "half Roman, half like the Knave of Hearts." Pound also proposes to use the "meditative, semi-dramatic, semi-epic" form of *Sordello*.

In *Sordello*, Browning had one man, Sordello, against whom to focus his "catch," and the Victorians had a set of beliefs. In Pound's "beastly and cantankerous age" doctrine is elusive and contradictory. Who ought to be Pound's Sordello? He cannot be sure. Pound evokes earlier worlds — Tuscany, China, Egypt. He does not believe that re-created history is true — "take it all for lies." Nor are his own imaginings "reality." There is a plurality of worlds. What the artist creates are "worlds enough." Artists discover new ways of seeing as in Pound's own time. There are, for example, the paintings of Lewis and Picasso, reflecting "the new world about us." Pound later said there are three planes in the *Cantos*, the "permanent" represented by characteristics of the gods; the "recurrent" archetypal fictional characters like Odysseus, or real, like Sir Philip Sidney; and "casual," the trivial, accidental events that form no pattern or design.

Canto I ends with "So that:" and Canto II begins with "Hang it all, there can be but one *Sordello!*" Browning takes his place with the many authors and texts Pound will cite.

Pound and Browning continue the descent into Hades introduced by Odysseus in Canto I. In *The Spirit of Romance*, Pound wrote, "Ovid, before Browning, raises the dead and dissects their mental processes; he walks with the people of myth." In *Make It New* Pound described Canto I as a close translation from the *Odyssey*.

Pound has also pointed out that the language of Canto II is, like the language of *Sordello*, highly charged. "The artist seeks out the luminous detail and presents it. He does not comment."

In the new Canto I, Odysseus symbolizes the male, active, and intelligent, and Aphrodite the female, stimulant to creative action. Canto II develops these themes. Sordello is looked upon in different ways, in Browning's mind, in Pound's, and in the finished work *Sordello*. The focus shifts to So-shu, a demi-urge in Chinese mythology. The scene fades into yet another, and a seal appears: the seal is feminine, it suggests the human; and, strangely, its eyes are the eyes of Picasso. Patterns recur. Eleanor of Aquitaine is like Helen of Troy, who is like Aphrodite, who is like Atalanta. The waves cover a new scene — and other metamorphoses take place. These changes come about as Pound thinks of a passage in the *Iliad* or *Odyssey*, or a Noh drama. A new image lights up, frequently emerging from the shadows of an ancient book. One character suggests another. A Greek waterscape suggests an Irish waterscape. A tree suggests Daphne. Always there is flow. New identities emerge and fade. Pound loves to work variations on the old myths. His imagination responds to them, as it almost never does — except in anger or contempt — to the civilization around him.

In Canto III, Pound remembers his stay in Venice in 1908, in his self-imposed exile. It was there he paid to have *A Lume Spento* printed. Pound recalls (this first appeared in the June 1917 Canto

1) his own visit to Venice, eyeing young Italian girls, as Browning had, and eating hard rolls for breakfast —

> So, for what it's worth,
> I have my background;
> And you had your background . . .

The Fourth Canto was published in forty copies on Japanese vellum by John Rodker in October 1919. In America it appeared in the *Dial* for June 1920. Canto IV is interesting if only because the literary allusions show how profoundly Pound's culture is the culture of books. In this Canto there is an allusion to Pindar, another to Catullus, yet another to the swallow Itys, and this suggests a similar tale by one of the troubadours, and so on.

Culture, for Pound, is the Mediterranean basin, especially in antiquity, with brief visits to the Renaissance or times long ago in Japan or China. The scenes evoked are like the winter dreams of a literary man with special interests in the classics, Provençal poetry, the Japanese Noh, and Chinese poetry. And the metamorphoses provide a constant discovery of the vitality in the old tales and a temporary stasis in a world of flux. They also provide escape from the dismal realities of the twentieth century.

In *It Was the Nightingale,* Ford Madox Ford said Pound's move to Paris was caused by Pound's challenging Lascelles Abercrombie to a duel. Abercrombie had written a piece for the *Times Literary Supplement,* favoring Milton. Prior to this he had enraged Pound by successfully running a magazine, *New Numbers,* in which he printed Georgian poetry. After his challenge, according to Ford, Pound was visited by the police. Another version of the story is that Abercrombie suggested they bombard each other with unsold copies of their books. In either case, Pound's ire would not be easily soothed. Shortly thereafter Pound took up residence in Paris.

Paris was soon to have a great deal of literary excitement, because of the presence of Joyce, Gertrude Stein, Ford, Hemingway, F. Scott Fitzgerald, Proust, Aragon, Cocteau, and many others. Pound was involved with some of these writers. He also continued to contribute to various magazines, and did a Paris letter for the *Dial*. And in Paris he could more easily live his role as aesthete. Margaret Anderson, for whose *Little Review* Pound was foreign editor, recalls his wearing a velvet beret, a flowing tie, and an emerald on his earlobe! He seemed more at home in Paris, but he did not give up all the relationships he had established in London. For example, his relationship with Joyce entered a new and, for Joyce, a very significant phase.

Pound's "discovery" of Joyce had come about as a result of his asking Joyce — who was struggling against poverty and suffering the refusal of printers to handle *Dubliners* — for permission to reprint "I hear an army charging upon the land" in *Des Imagistes*. As advisory editor for the *Egoist*, edited by Dora Marsden and later Harriet Weaver, he had asked for work in prose. Joyce sent the opening of *A Portrait of the Artist as a Young Man*. It was accepted, and, following a generous advance to Joyce, the novel ran serially in the *Egoist*. At the end of 1913, thanks to Pound, Joyce found himself in the very middle of a literary revolution. While the *Portrait* was still being serialized, *Dubliners* finally appeared, and Pound reviewed it, saying Joyce had earned a place for himself "among English contemporary prose writers."

From Paris, Pound advised Joyce to join him. Joyce wrote a letter (July 1, 1920) saying, "My address in Paris will be chez M. Ezra Pound, Hotel de l'Elysée, rue de Beaune 9." Temperamentally the two men were unlike and did not make easy companions — but they remained friendly. Joyce never forgot Pound's generosity. And when he was broadcasting over Rome radio during the war Pound devoted one talk to celebrating Joyce's career.

In Paris Pound also continued his relationship with Eliot. On one, now famous, occasion, Pound blue-penciled the poem that would be published as *The Waste Land*. "It was in 1922 [1921]," Eliot has written, "that I placed before him in Paris the manuscript of a sprawling chaotic poem called The Waste Land, which left his hands about half its size, in the form in which it appears in print." If Eliot ever causes the earlier version to be published, readers can then judge the rightness or wrongness of his admiration for Pound's performance as editor.

In Paris, Pound also continued his relationship with Ford, who later recalled Pound's sponsoring the music of George Antheil, and taking up sculpture. "Mr. Pound fiercely struck blocks of granite with sledge hammers." Pound told Ford he had little time for literature, but he did help Ford to get John Quinn, a New York philanthropist, to subsidize the short-lived *Transatlantic Review* and also helped get contributions. Pound introduced Ford to Ernest Hemingway, who had submitted his stories to Pound's blue pencil. Pound was ballyhooing him as a magnificent new writer. As one might expect, Gertrude Stein, Hemingway's other mentor, and Pound were not ardent admirers of each other. Miss Stein called him a "village explainer" and he called her "a charming old fraud."

In 1923, Pound and Hemingway toured Italian battlefields. Hemingway explained the strategy of a Renaissance soldier of fortune, Sigismondo de Malatesta. The trip was the beginning of Pound's decision to live in Italy, and in Malatesta he found a new hero for glorification in the *Cantos*.

Sigismondo de Malatesta, warrior, schemer, passionate male, and lover of beauty, delighted Pound. Malatesta must have been full of guile and a violent man even to survive in the political struggles in which he contested, with Pius II and other feudal monarchs, but in honoring his powers as an opportunist Pound jauntily shapes fifteenth-century Italian history to suit his own purposes. His use of letters and documents gives his "history" (in Cantos VIII, IX, and X) an air of being a disinterested glimpse of a thoroughly great man, Sigismondo Malatesta.

Clearly what endeared Malatesta to Pound was that he left behind him, although unfinished, a beautiful building, the Tempio. Sword in hand, standing neck deep in a marsh, or despoiling a city, Malatesta carried a dream in his head.

Considering his earlier productivity, Pound published little during his Paris period. He had, however, discovered Malatesta. And a look at *A Draft of XVI Cantos*, published soon after he moved to Rapallo, shows that he had discovered another cultural hero, Kung, or in the Latinized version of his name, Confucius. (Pound had acquainted himself with James Legge's twenty-eight volumes of *Chinese Classics*, 1861–86.) Mostly he refers to *The Analects* and *The Unwobbling Pivot* and the *Great Digest*, later translated by him under these titles.

Confucius had gained a reputation as a philosopher prime minister of Lu, but he resigned in 495 B.C. when the monarch gave himself to pleasure, and he visited other states as a teacher. Confucius, in Pound's words, said such things as "If a man does not discipline himself he cannot bring discipline into his home," and "One courteous family can lift a whole state into courtesy."

A difficulty in reading Canto XIII and others like it is that one cannot understand the allusions, for example the elliptical conversation Confucius has in one village or another, unless one knows the context from which Pound took them.

Occasionally there are lovely passages in the *Cantos*, but increasingly Ezra Pound becomes less and less the poet bent on creating new images and identities, and more and more the insistent teacher.

After some months of indecision, Pound and his wife settled in Rapallo, a seaside village on the Italian Riviera. It has been described by Yeats, who took up residence there in 1929: "Mountains that shelter the bay from all but the strongest wind, bare brown branches of low vines and of tall trees blurring their outline as though with a soft mist; houses mirrored in an almost motionless sea . . . The little town described in An Ode on a Grecian Urn." There Pound lived for twenty years, until his arrest by American troops, following his indictment for treason. Occasionally he visited Paris and London, but mostly remained in Rapallo. The dramatist Gerhart Hauptmann lived there in the summer, and visitors included Aldington, Ford, Antheil, Max Beerbohm, and others. Pound occasionally had disciples living nearby. Knowing him to be a famous poet, the townspeople treated him deferentially.

One might expect the quiet town and the almost motionless sea to have helped Pound write more *Cantos* in which Ovidian nymphs were pursued by ardent young swains, and there are some such *Cantos*. But there are many more in which he quarrels with America, its culture and universities, but especially its economy and banking system.

Pound believed that a good government was possible only when the state controlled money. This was best done, for the good of all of the people, by a benevolent dictator, like Mussolini. Other ideal "dictators," as seen by Pound, are Jefferson, Adams, Jackson, Confucius, a Chinese ruler, Quang-Ngau-chè, and others. Another wise ruler, according to Pound, was Martin Van Buren, and he implies there has been a conspiracy, at least of stupidity, to keep his *Autobiography* untaught in American universities.

Pound's objections to American capitalism derive from his belief that a man should be rewarded according to the worth of his work. Under our "leisure class" society, one makes money by

37

manipulating money, not by producing worthwhile products or beautiful artifacts. Thus the many references in the *Cantos* to usury.

In Rapallo, Pound appears to have read certain works in an obsessive way; for example, the works of John Adams. About eighty pages of the *Cantos* deal with Adams. As he had in the Malatesta *Cantos*, Pound quotes endlessly, transcribing phrases. Malatesta, however, was partially transformed and lives as a fictional creation. Adams is lost in the transcription from his own writings.

At one period, Pound seemed ready to give up literature. Salvation was to be found only in economics, in the writings of Douglas, Gesell, and Orage. In a letter written in 1934, Yeats reported that Pound "would talk nothing but politics. . . . He urged me to read the works of Captain Douglas who alone knew what caused our suffering. He took away my manuscript ["King of the Clock Tower"] and went away denouncing Dublin as 'a reactionary hole' because I had said that I was reading Shakespeare, would go on to Chaucer, and found all that I wanted of modern life in 'detection and the wild West.' Next day his judgment came and that in a single word 'Putrid.' "

In addition to his explaining the nature of economics and politics to the English-speaking world, Pound had been explaining the ABC's of reading and how to read. In the New York *Herald Tribune Books* he wrote: "The great writers need no debunking. The pap is not in them and doesn't need to be squeezed out. They do not lend themselves to imperial and sentimental exploitations. A civilization was founded on Homer, civilization not a mere bloated empire. The Macedonian domination rose and grew after the sophists. It also subsided." In such an article, Pound sometimes makes acute observations, but the sentences and paragraphs are often discrete, and the author seems distracted and unsure of the unifying idea of his discourse. There is also a disturbing immaturity and naiveté in Pound's pronouncements: "Really one DON'T need to know a language. One NEEDS, damn well needs, to know the few hundred words in the few really good poems that any language has in it." Or "It takes about 600 to make a civilization."

Pound's prose works during the late 1920's and the 1930's reveal that he repeated many things he had said earlier, and that he continued his engagement with America. His slangy wit gradually grows cruder, and his vulgarity coarser.

In 1930, the Black Sun Press of Caresse Crosby issued his *Imaginary Letters*. Some of these were written during his London period, and some of them were from later years. In one of the letters, he says he is told Russia is much like America. He infers that both are "barbarous" countries. In another, he says he hopes "to hear the last of these Russians," adding that the talk about the Russian soul bores him silly — "The Russian (large R, definite article, Artzibasheff, Bustikosseff, Slobingobski, Spititoutski and Co. Amalgamated, communatated, etc.). 'The Russian,' my dear Caroline, is nothing but the western European with his conning-tower or his top-layer . . . removed. . . . Civilized man, *any* civilized man who has a normal lining to his stomach, may become Russian for the price of a little mixed alcohol, or of, perhaps a good deal of mixed alcohol, but it is a matter of shillings, not a matter of dynamic attainment. Once, and perhaps only once, have I been drunk enough to feel like a Russian. Try it, my dearest young lady, try it. Try it and clear your mind, free your life from this obsession of Russians (if Lenin and Co. have not freed you.)"

In a letter on the language of Joyce and modern literature at its best, he says: "The author [of an article he is citing] says, and I think with reason, that wherever Joyce has made use of lice, or dung, or other disgusting unpleasantness he has done so with the intention, and with, as a considerable artist, the result of heightening some effect of beauty, or twisting tighter some intensity." He calls this Joyce's "metal finish." It is, he says, similar to his own "sterilized surgery." Shortly he adds, as an example of his own "vigour," a "fairly Baudelairian but . . . nowhere inevitable" sonnet of his, or rather the two stanzas he can recall:

> One night stretched out along a hebrew bitch —
> Like two corpses at the undertakers —
> This carcass, sold alike to jews and quakers
> Reminded me of beauty noble and rich.

These lines are not unlike those to be found in many of the later *Cantos*. Pound is like a small boy writing dirty verses on the lavatory wall. Pound's comments indicate he knew he had not written a successful poem, but he seems not to have recognized the shocking crassness of which he was capable.

From Rapallo, Pound sent out his advice to the world, especially to his "fellow 'Muricans." One such piece of advice is called *ABC of Reading*. It was published by an American university press, Yale. "How to Study Poetry," two prefatory paragraphs, never mentions poetry — or the study of poetry. "Warning," a kind of introduction, contains seven paragraphs, each about a different subject. In Section One, Chapter One, he says our way of looking at objects should be more scientific; we should emulate the biologist who compares one specimen with another. Then he discusses Fenollosa's *Essay on the Chinese Written Character*, adding that organized university life in America and England had made it almost impossible for him to get the essay published. Next he says medieval man wasn't as victimized by terminology as we are. He then returns to Fenollosa, and presents the Chinese picture words or images for man, tree, sun, and sun in the tree's branches, meaning the East. Fenollosa, he continues, demonstrated that the Chinese "word" or "ideogram" for "red is based on something everyone KNOWS." The implication seems to be that the English word *red* is based on knowledge no one has or experience no one has had! In Section Two we are told about Laboratory Condition — that is, that experiencing art is preferable to hearing discussions of it. To make this point, Pound lists the programs played by several "serious musicians" on one occasion in Rapallo, adding that the best volume of musical criticism he has ever encountered is Boris De Schloezer's *Stravinsky*. Lastly there is "The Ideogrammic Method or the Method of Science." In these paragraphs he mentions neither ideograms nor scientific methods. He says you cannot prevent Mr. Buggins from preferring a painting by Carlo Dolci to one by Cosimo Tura, but if you have them next to each other "you can very seriously impede his setting up a false tradition. . . ." Finally he says that a middle-aged man knows the *rightness* of what he knows. A young man may be right, but he doesn't know *how* right he may be.

The chapter says almost nothing, and is wildly incoherent. Certainly a writer lacking Pound's reputation, ironically a reputation as a great explicator, would not have stood a chance of having a publisher accept this book. If an academic adviser had received such a chapter as the opening of a candidate's M.A. thesis he would have been obligated to dismiss it as the gibberish it is. *ABC of Reading* reads like the comments of an ex-schoolmaster who has been bereft of his senses. One reading an occasional sentence might feel that the ex-schoolmaster was only mad north-northeast, but reading it entire makes clear that this is the work of a deranged mind.

Another of these strange volumes was published in England as *Guide to Kulchur*, and in the United States as *Culture*. The same subjects recur. There are discussions of Confucius, Vorticism, tradition, textbooks, Provençal poets, the nature of first-rate novels, decline of the Adams family, etc., etc. Typically, "Tradition" examines several discrete subjects, none of them especially illuminating. It opens with a discussion of Frobenius, one of Pound's heroes. He quotes several tags from antiquity, refers to Confucian harmonies, Madame Tussaud's, an unnamed general, etc. Pound is telling the reader that he can understand his own culture only if he understands some other culture. *"I am not, in these slight memories, merely 'pickin' daisies.' A man does not know his own ADDRESS (in time) until he knows where his own time and milieu stand in relation to other times and conditions."* But the "slight memories" Pound recounts are mostly empty prattling. For example, he mentions a book entitled *With the Empress Dowager of China* by K. A. Carl. "This book," he says, "records a high degree of civilization." Then these sentences follow, in the same paragraph. "Fenollosa is said to have been the second European to be able to take part in a Noh performance. The whole civilization reflected in Noh is a high civilization." Individually the three sentences make a kind of sense. In sequence they make no sense. Nor do they make sense in terms of the paragraphs preceding them, or the paragraphs that follow.

It needs to be said that Pound's prose in these books, as well as in his economic and political pamphlets, is quite as disordered as the phrases and sentences in the later *Cantos*. Some critics have rationalized the fragmented passages of the *Cantos* as a new "poetic strategy." The truth would seem to be that Pound was no longer capable of the kind of coherence he had sometimes achieved as a young man.

In the *Cantos*, as the years pass, there is an increasing dependence on violence and shock, on obscenities and scatological descriptions. Worse, there is an airy indifference when Pound mentions genocide or mass suffering. F. R. Leavis, an early admirer of Pound's contributions as poet, critic, and man of letters, has said,

"The spectacle of Pound's degeneration is a terrible one, and no one ought to pretend that it is anything but what it is."

Pound returned to the United States in 1939; received an honorary degree from Hamilton College; and went to Washington where he talked with Senator Borah, Secretary of Agriculture Wallace, and others, attempting to prove to them that a change in economic policies would avert war. Back in Italy when the war began, he broadcast over Rome radio, attacking Roosevelt's policies. After Pearl Harbor, when Pound and his wife tried to leave Italy, an unidentified American official refused them permission to board a diplomatic train leaving Rome. Shortly he resumed his broadcasts. As a series they are undoubtedly the most curious efforts at propaganda ever allowed over a national radio. Pound talked about London as he had known it, E. E. Cummings, Joyce, Chinese philosophy, economics, and his own *Cantos*. No wonder the Italians suspected him of being an American agent. But the United States attorney general asked for his indictment, and when the Americans reached Genoa, in northern Italy, Pound gave himself up.

Imprisoned at Pisa in the summer of 1945, under harsh circumstances, he suffered hallucinations and a collapse. After medical care, he was treated more humanely and resumed his writing. In November he was flown to Washington. Eventually he was committed to St. Elizabeth's, a federal hospital for the insane, and remained there until the United States dropped its indictment thirteen years later, when he returned to Italy.

During this period he continued to write pamphlets, contribute *Cantos* to various magazines — and generally repeat the same opinions he had expressed in his broadcasts.

Much of the writing from this period is rant, fustion, and bombast, but there are two partial exceptions, *The Pisan Cantos*, for which he received the Bollingen Award (which fluttered literary dovecotes and caused several angry editorials), and *Women of Trachis*, a translation from Sophocles. In *The Pisan Cantos* there are occasional beautiful phrases, but there is no evidence that Pound had recovered the clarity of vision and metaphorical powers of the early *Cantos*. *The Pisan Cantos* are, like his radio talks, filled with discrete observations, and *non sequiturs*. But there is also a new dimension.

He thinks back over his life in London, France, and Rapallo, and recalls what Ford, or Yeats, or Hemingway, or whoever, had said. Pound the aesthete has disappeared and Pound the preacher appears only intermittently. There is an awareness of human anguish, of ancient folly, and of Pound's own vanity.

> If the hoar frost grip thy tent
> Thou wilt give thanks when night is spent.

The Pisan Cantos are the disordered work of a man who has been through hell.

In *Women of Trachis*, Pound achieves something like the immediacy of language that he achieved in "Propertius." Where Lewis Campbell has

> Dear child, dear boy! even from the lowliest head
> Wise counsel may come forth.

(he is referring to wise advice coming from a slave), Pound says:

> See here, son, this slave talks sense,
> more than some free folks.

It's the American idiom, but probably a lot closer to Sophocles' intent than is Campbell's idiom. *Women of Trachis* is a remarkable performance when set against some of Pound's ranting prose.

How should one view the life and career of Ezra Pound? Several eminent writers, including Yeats, Eliot, and Hemingway, have stated their indebtedness to him. Without doubt he was a catalytic agent in many of the movements associated with modernism.

As for his place as a poet, posterity will decide. Current critical estimates are diverse and irreconcilable. What Auden had to say about Yeats applies to Pound:

> Time that is intolerant
> Of the brave and innocent,
> And indifferent in a week
> To a beautiful physique,
>
> Worships language and forgives
> Everyone by whom it lives;
> Pardons cowardice, conceit,
> Lays its honours at their feet.

Presumably Time will forgive or at least forget the offenses or errors of Ezra Pound. If his poetry achieves a place in the permanent canon of English and American poetry, Time, as Auden says, will lay its honors at his feet.

◢ Selected Bibliography

Selected Works of Ezra Pound

Pound has published such a large number of books and contributed to so many collections, anthologies, and magazines that a full listing of his works would fill many pages. The titles listed below are intended to suggest the variety of his writing.

A Lume Spento. Venice: A. Antonini, 1908. (Limited edition.)

Personæ of Ezra Pound. London: Elkin Mathews, 1909.

Exultations of Ezra Pound. London: Elkin Mathews, 1909.

The Spirit of Romance. London: Dent, 1910.

Provença: Poems Selected from Personæ, Exultations, and Canzoniere of Ezra Pound. Boston: Small, Maynard, 1910.

Canzoni of Ezra Pound. London: Elkin Mathews, 1911.

The Ripostes of Ezra Pound Whereunto Are Appended the Complete Poetical Works of T. E. Hulme, with Prefatory Note. London: Swift, 1912.

Des Imagistes: An Anthology of the Imagists, edited by Ezra Pound. New York: Boni, 1914; London: Poetry Book Shop, 1914.

"Homage to Wilfrid Blunt," *Poetry,* 3:220–23 (March 1914).

"Vorticism," *Fortnightly Review,* 102:461–71 (September 1914).

'Noh,' or Accomplishment: A Study of the Classical Stage of Japan (with Ernest Fenollosa). London: Macmillan, 1916; New York: Knopf, 1917.

Gaudier-Brzeska: A Memoir. London: John Lane, 1916. (Reissued, New York: New Directions, 1960.)

Certain Noble Plays of Japan, from the manuscripts of Ernest Fenollosa, chosen and finished by Ezra Pound. Churchtown, Dundrum: Cuala Press, 1916.

Lustra of Ezra Pound. London: Elkin Mathews, 1916; New York: Knopf, 1917.

Review of *Ernest Dowson* by Victor Plarr, *Poetry,* 6:43–45 (April 1915).

"T. S. Eliot," *Poetry,* 10:264–71 (August 1917). (Review of *Prufrock and Other Observations* by T. S. Eliot.)

"Irony, Laforgue, and Some Satire," *Poetry,* 11:93–98 (November 1917).

Pavannes and Divisions. New York: Knopf, 1918.

"The Hard and the Soft in French Poetry," *Poetry,* 11:264–71 (February 1918).

The Natural Philosophy of Love by Remy de Gourmont, translated by Ezra Pound. New York: Boni and Liveright, 1922.

A Draft of XVI Cantos of Ezra Pound. Paris: Three Mountains Press, 1924 or 1925. (Limited edition.)

46

Selected Bibliography

Personæ: The Collected Poems of Ezra Pound. New York: Boni and Liveright, 1926. (Reprinted with additional poems, New York: New Directions, 1949.)

Imaginary Letters. Paris: Black Sun Press, 1930. (Limited edition.)

ABC of Reading. London: Routledge, 1934; New Haven: Yale University Press, 1934.

Jefferson and/or Mussolini. London: Nott, 1935; New York: Liveright, 1936.

Polite Essays. London: Faber and Faber, 1937; Norfolk, Conn.: New Directions, 1939.

Guide to Kulchur. London: Faber and Faber, 1938; (as *Culture*) Norfolk, Conn.: New Directions, 1938.

The Pisan Cantos. New York: New Directions, 1948.

The Cantos of Ezra Pound. New York: New Directions, 1948. (Cantos 1–71 and 74–84.)

Selected Poems. New York: New Directions, 1949.

Section: Rock-Drill: 85–95 de los cantares. New York: New Directions, 1949.

Money pamphlets. 6 vols. London: Peter Russell, 1950–52. (These were published earlier in Italy.)

The Letters of Ezra Pound, edited by T. D. D. Paige. New York: Harcourt, Brace, 1950.

Patria Mia. Chicago: R. F. Seymour, 1950.

The Translations of Ezra Pound, edited by Hugh Kenner. New York: New Directions, 1954.

Literary Essays, edited by T. S. Eliot. New York: New Directions, 1954.

The Classic Anthology Defined by Confucius. Cambridge, Mass.: Harvard University Press, 1954.

Women of Trachis by Sophocles, translated by Ezra Pound. London: Neville Spearman, 1956.

Thrones: 96–109 de los cantares. New York: New Directions, 1959.

Impact. Chicago: Regnery, 1960.

Current American Reprints

ABC of Reading. New York: New Directions. $1.35.

Classic Noh Theatre of Japan (with Ernest Fenollosa). New York: New Directions. $1.25.

The Confucian Odes. New York: New Directions. $1.45.

Love Poems of Ancient Egypt, translated by Ezra Pound and Noel Stock. New York: New Directions. $1.50.

Natural Philosophy of Love by Remy de Gourmont, translated by Ezra Pound. New York: Collier. $.95.

Selected Poems. New York: New Directions. $1.35.

Bibliographical Aids

Edwards, John, comp. *A Preliminary Checklist of the Writings of Ezra Pound.* New Haven: Kirgo-Books, 1953.

Edwards, John, and W. W. Vasse, eds. *Annotated Index to the Cantos of Ezra Pound.* Berkeley: University of California Press, 1958.

Critical and Biographical Studies

Blackmur, R. P. *Language as Gesture.* New York: Harcourt, Brace, 1952.

Edwards, John, ed. *The Pound Newsletter.* Berkeley: University of California, 1954–56.

Elliott, George P. "On Pound — Poet of Many Voices," *Carleton Miscellany,* 2:79–103 (Summer 1961). (Published at Carleton College, Northfield, Minn.)

Emery, Clark. *Ideas into Action: A Study of Pound's Cantos.* Coral Gables, Fla.: University of Miami Press, 1958.

Espey, John. *Ezra Pound's Mauberley; A Study in Composition.* Berkeley: University of California Press, 1955.

Kenner, Hugh. *The Poetry of Ezra Pound.* New York: New Directions, 1951.

Leary, Lewis, ed. *Motive and Method in the Cantos of Ezra Pound.* New York: Columbia University Press, 1954.

Leavis, F. R. *New Bearings in English Poetry.* London: Chatto and Windus, 1932.

Mayo, Robert, ed. *The Analyst.* Evanston, Ill.: Northwestern University (Department of English), 1953–date. (Various scholars annotate the *Cantos* in this publication, which appears at intervals.)

Miner, Earl. *The Japanese Tradition in British and American Literature.* Princeton: Princeton University Press, 1958.

Mullins, Eustace. *This Difficult Individual, Ezra Pound.* New York: Fleet, 1961.

Norman, Charles. *Ezra Pound.* New York: Macmillan, 1960.

O'Connor, William Van, and Edward Stone, eds. *A Casebook on Ezra Pound.* New York: Crowell, 1959.

Putnam, Samuel. *Paris Was Our Mistress.* New York: Viking, 1947.

Quarterly Review of Literature, Ezra Pound Issue, vol. 5, no. 2 (1949). (Published at Bard College, Annandale, New York.)

Quinn, Sister M. Bernetta. *The Metamorphic Tradition in Modern Poetry.* New Brunswick, N.J.: Rutgers University Press, 1955.

Rosenthal, M. L. *A Primer of Ezra Pound.* New York: Macmillan, 1960.

Russell, Peter, ed. *An Examination of Ezra Pound.* New York: New Directions, 1950.

Wright, George. *The Poet in the Poem* Berkeley: University of California Press, 1960